Sous Vide Cookbook:

101 Modern yet Simple Techniques for Rich, Healthy and Delicious Sous Vide Home Cooking

Evelyn Halliday

Table of Contents

Introduction

Welcome to **Sous Vide Cookbook: 101 Modern yet Simple Techniques for Rich, Healthy and Delicious Sous Vide Home Cooking**, the second book from **The Sadistically Delicious Series.** I would like to thank you for choosing this book to aid you in your journey to becoming a culinary mastermind. **The Sadistically Delicious Series** was designed with the goal of helping others to get professional results from their home kitchen appliances every time. This book, the Second in the series is dedicated to Sous Vide cooking. If you have an interest in air fryer cooking take a look at the first book in the series, **Air Fryer Cookbook, 101 Simple and Delicious Air Fryer Recipes for Fantastic Food Fast**. Remember to keep your eyes peeled for the third book in the series **Pressure Cooker Cookbook** coming soon.

This book was written in order to give absolutely anyone all the information they need to cook gourmet Sous Vide meals at home. Sous Vide are fantastic as they not only prepare healthy meals they also greatly enhance flavours. Sous Vide cooking is becoming extremely popular of late due to its simplicity and ability to provide reliable, high quality results. These amazing machines have gained their reputation by combining technology and proven cooking techniques, all of which can be used within the home. For example, by setting the exact temperature for rare/medium/medium-well or well-done on the Sous Vide anyone can cook the perfect steak, every time.

A few of the other benefits of Sous Vide cooking are:

- Healthier meals, Sous Vide cooking locks in the goodness

- Food is cooked precisely and evenly

- Small sleek designs allow for easy storage

- Temperature control features stop food from burning

- Make your day easier by setting your Sous Vide in the morning, and return from work to a perfectly cooked meal

I hope you enjoy and are inspired by the recipes within.

Best wishes

Evelyn Halliday

Recommended Sous Vide Models

Anova Precision Cooker Bluetooth & WI-FI 220v UK Plug

The Anova Precision Cooker Bluetooth & WI-FI is a well-made and reliable machine. Its sleek design is quickly making this model a kitchen must have. This model can be controlled via Bluetooth technology, making changes to settings both quick and easy. This model will also send alerts to your mobile phone when your dish is ready. Other great benefits of this model are its low power consumption and digital screen.

Anova Culinary Bluetooth Precision Cooker (Black)

This Anova model is one of the few Sous Vide that has an easy to read screen displaying exact water temperature. The removable clamp means this Sous Vide can fit any water bath or pan. The simple to use control wheel makes setting adjustments easy. Throw a Steak in at 120°F for 2 hours for perfection.

Wancle Sous Vide Precision Cooker Immersion Circulator (Black)

This popular model of Sous Vide does not require a Vacuum Sealer to use neither does it require a large bath container as it will fit to practically any pot. The water temperature is kept consistent. Reliability is paramount with Sous Vide cooking and the Wancle Sous Vide Precision Cooker is without a doubt one of the best.

BEEF DISHES

Steak Medium Well

Ingredients

- Steak(s) of your choice

- Salt and Ground Black Pepper to taste

- Dry Rub Steak Marinade (Optional)

Method

1. Season the Steak with Salt and Ground Black Pepper to taste and Dry Rub Steak Marinade.

2. Seal the Steak by vacuum sealer or the water displacement method.

Cooking your Steak Medium Well

1. Pre-heat the Sous Vide to 145°F (140°F for medium).

2. Cook the Steak for 60 minutes.

3. Remove the Steaks from the Sous Vide and Seer in a pan.

Serving

Serve with a sprinkling of Salt and Ground Black Pepper to taste and Green Salad.

Steak Medium Rare

Ingredients

- Steak(s) of your choice

- Salt and Ground Black Pepper to taste

- Dry Rub Steak Marinade (Optional)

Method

1. Season the Steak with Salt and Ground Black Pepper to taste and Dry Rub Steak Marinade.

2. Seal the Steak by vacuum sealer or the water displacement method.

Cooking your Steak Medium Rare

1. Pre-heat the Sous Vide to 130°F (120°F for rare).

2. Cook the Steak for 60 minutes.

3. Remove the Steaks from the Sous Vide and Seer in a pan.

Serving

Serve with a sprinkling of Salt and Ground Black Pepper to taste and Green Salad.

T-Bone Steak

Ingredients

- 2 Large T-bone Steaks

- 2 Sprigs of Rosemary

- 2 Sprigs of Thyme

- 1 Clove of Garlic finely chopped

- Salt and Ground Black Pepper to taste

- Olive Oil

Method

1. Season the T-bone Steaks with Salt and Ground Black Pepper and then seal the T-bones Steaks, Rosemary, Thyme by vacuum sealer or the water displacement method.

Cooking your T-bone steak

1. Pre-heat the Sous Vide to:

   - 130°F for Medium Rare.

   - 144°F for Medium.

   - 152°F for Medium Well.

2. Cook the T-bones Steaks for 60 minutes.

3. Warm some Olive Oil in a Frying pan on a medium-high heat and add the chopped Garlic.

4. Remove the T-bone Steaks from the Sous Vide and sear both sides in the Frying Pan.

Serving

Serve with a sprinkling of Salt and Ground Black Pepper to taste and Green Salad.

Tenderloins

Ingredients

- 2 Medium Tenderloins

- 2 Sprigs of Rosemary

- 2 Sprigs of Thyme

- 1 Clove of Garlic finely chopped

- Salt and Ground Black Pepper to taste

- Olive Oil

Method

1. Season the Tenderloins with Salt and Ground Black Pepper and then seal the Tenderloins, Rosemary, Thyme by vacuum sealer or the water displacement method.

Cooking your Tenderloins

1. Pre-heat the Sous Vide to:

  - 130°F for Medium Rare.

  - 144°F for Medium.

  - 152°F for Medium Well.

2. Cook the Tenderloins for 60 minutes.

3. Warm some Olive Oil in a Frying pan on a medium-high heat and add the chopped Garlic.

4. Remove the Tenderloins from the Sous Vide and sear both sides in the Frying Pan.

Serving

Serve with a sprinkling of Salt and Ground Black Pepper to taste and Green Salad.

Strip Steak

Ingredients

- 1 Large Strip Steak

- 2 Sprigs of Rosemary

- 2 Sprigs of Thyme

- 1 Clove of Garlic finely chopped

- Salt and Ground Black Pepper to taste

- Olive Oil

Method

1. Season the Strip Steak with Salt and Ground Black Pepper and then seal the Strip Steak, Rosemary, Thyme by vacuum sealer or the water displacement method.

Cooking your Strip Steak

1. Pre-heat the Sous Vide to:

    - 132°F for Medium Rare.

    - 146°F for Medium.

    - 156°F for Medium Well.

2. Cook the Strip Steak for 90 minutes.

3. Warm some Olive Oil in a Frying pan on a medium-high heat and add the chopped Garlic.

4. Remove the Strip Steak from the Sous Vide and sear both sides in the Frying Pan.

Serving

Serve with a sprinkling of Salt and Ground Black Pepper to taste and Green Salad.

Sous Vide Butter Steak and Asparagus

Ingredients

- Sirloin or Fillet Steaks

- 125g Fresh Asparagus

- Olive Oil

- Salt and Ground Black Pepper to taste

- 2 Teaspoons of Butter

Method

1. Season the Steaks with Salt and Ground Black Pepper to taste.

2. Seal the Steaks, Asparagus and Butter by vacuum sealer or the water displacement method.

Cooking your Sous Vide Butter Steak and Asparagus

1. Pre-heat the Sous Vide to 146°F.

2. Cook the Butter Steaks and Asparagus for 90 minutes.

3. Warm some Olive Oil in a Frying Pan or Griddle on a medium-high heat.

4. Remove the Butter Steaks and Asparagus from the Sous Vide, drain any excess liquid and place the Steaks and Asparagus in the Pan for 4 minutes turning midway.

Serving

Serve hot with Fries/Chips.

Cheeseburgers

Ingredients

- 600g Minced Beef

- 1 Onion very finely chopped

- 1 Clove of Garlic very finely chopped

- 1 Egg lightly whisked

- 1 Teaspoon of Horseradish Sauce

- 1 Heaped teaspoon of Tomato Puree

- 1 Teaspoon of Mixed Herbs

- Salt and Ground Pepper to taste

Method

1. Thoroughly mix all of the ingredients in a bowl and leave to rest in the fridge for 10 minutes.

2. Remove from the fridge and, using your hands shape the mix into 6-8 Burgers and return to the fridge for a further 10 minutes.

Cooking your Cheeseburgers

1. Pre-heat the Sous Vide to 150°F.

2. Cook the Burgers for 30 minutes

3. Remove Burgers from the Sous Vide and place on the Grill or Barbecue for 2 minutes before turning, adding a slice of cheese and cooking for a further minutes.

Serving

Serve with Burger Buns, Fries, Ketchup and Mustard.

Beer Brisket

Ingredients

- 1 Kilo of Flat Cut Brisket

- 1 Large White Onion, chopped

- 1 Tablespoon of Dijon Mustard

- 2 Tablespoons of Brown Sugar

- 1 Tablespoon of Honey

- 1 Teaspoon of Salt

- 2 Teaspoons of Ground Black Pepper

- Olive Oil

Method

1. Warm some Olive Oil in a Frying Pan, Skillet or Griddle on a medium-high heat.

2. Season the Brisket with a little Salt and Ground Black Pepper to taste and sear the Brisket, fat side down cooking for 4-6 minutes.

3. Place the Brisket to one side and toss the Onions in the Pan, cooking for 2 minutes or until they begin to brown.

4. Pour the beer into the Pan along with the Sugar, Honey, Dijon Mustard, Salt and Ground Black Pepper.

5. Seal the Brisket and Beer Marinade in a Sous Vide bag and seal by the water displacement method.

Cooking your Beer Brisket

1. Pre-heat the Sous Vide to 145°F.

2. Cook the Beer Brisket for 48 hours.

3. Remove the Beer Brisket from the Sous Vide and leave to sit for 10 minutes.

4. Pour the Beer Marinade into a Saucepan, place on a medium-high heat and stir until the Marinade has reduced by half (add Salt and Ground Black Pepper to taste).

5. Slice the Brisket.

Serving

Serve with Roasted Potatoes, Mixed Vegetables and pour on some of the Beer Marinade Sauce.

Salt and Pepper Brisket

Ingredients

- 1 Brisket, flat or point cut up to 2kg

- ¼ Cup Salt

- ¼ Fresh Ground Peppercorns

- 1 Tablespoon of Dried Rosemary

- 1 Tablespoon Dried Thyme

Method

1. Mix together the Salt, Ground Pepper, Dried Rosemary and Dried Thyme.

2. Generously and evenly coat the entire Brisket with the mix.

3. Seal the Brisket (cut in half if necessary) by vacuum sealer or the water displacement method.

Cooking your Salt and Pepper Brisket

1. Pre-heat the Sous Vide to 155°F.

2. Cook the Brisket for a minimum of 24 to 36 hours.

3. Once removed allow the Brisket to cool for around 60 minutes.

4. Pre-heat the oven to 300°F.

5. Give the Brisket another coating of the Salt, Pepper, Rosemary and Thyme mix, put the Brisket on a wire rack in a baking tray and place on the middle shelf in the oven.

6. Cook the Brisket for 1½-2 hours or until the outer crust darkens.

7. Remove the Brisket from the oven, cover with foil and leave to rest for 10-15 minutes before thinly slicing.

Serving

Serve with Mixed Vegetables and Roast Potatoes. Perfect for sandwiches.

Beef Bourguignon

Ingredients

- 800g Diced Beef

- 3 Slices of Bacon

- 1 Onion, chopped

- 2 Carrots, peeled and chopped

- 2 Cloves of Garlic

- ½ Bottle of Red Wine

- 1 Cup of Water

- 1 Teaspoon of Salt

- 1 Teaspoon of Ground Black Pepper

- 3 Tablespoons of Butter

- 400ml Beef Stock

- 1 Tablespoon of Tomato Puree

- 3 Sprigs of Rosemary

- 3 Sprigs of Thyme

- 2 Tablespoons of Flour

- Olive Oil

Method

1. Season the Beef with a little Salt and Ground Black Pepper to taste.

2. Toss the Beef in the Flour ensuring all the pieces are fully covered.

3. Warm some Olive Oil in a Frying Pan, throw in the Onions and cook for 2 minutes on a medium-high heat.

4. Add the Beef to the Onions and sear the meat.

5. Add the Carrots, Garlic, Rosemary, Thyme, Tomato Puree, Beef Stock, Water, Salt and Pepper to the Beef.

6. Using a Sous Vide Bag seal the Beef Bourguignon by the water displacement method.

Cooking your Beef Bourguignon

1. Pre-heat the Sous Vide to 140°F.

2. Cook the Beef Bourguignon for 20-24 hours.

3. Remove the Beef Bourguignon from the Sous Vide and serve.

CHICKEN DISHES

Chermoula Spiced Chicken

Ingredients

- 4-6 Chicken Breasts

- 3 Cloves of Garlic finely chopped

- 1 ½ Teaspoons Chermoula Spice Mix

- 1 Small handful of fresh Coriander, chopped

- 1 White Onion finely chopped

- Salt and Ground Black Pepper to taste

Method

1. In a bowl mix the Garlic, Chermoula Spice Mix, Coriander, Onion, Salt and Ground Black Pepper to taste.

2. Cut some slices into the chicken but be careful not to cut them all the way through. Coat the Chicken in the mix.

3. Seal the Chicken along with any remaining mix by vacuum sealer of the water displacement method.

Cooking your Chermoula Spiced chicken

1. Pre-heat the Sous Vide to 160°F.

2. Cook the Chicken for 2 hours.

Serving

Serve hot with Basmati Rice and a squeeze of Lemon Juice.

Honey and Lime Chicken

Ingredients

- 4-6 Chicken Breasts

- 2 Cloves of Garlic finely chopped

- 2 Tablespoons of Honey

- 2 Tablespoons of freshly squeezed Lime Juice

- 1 Pinch of Chili Flakes

- 2 Tablespoons of Olive Oil

- Salt and Ground Black Pepper to taste

Method

1. In a bowl mix the Honey, Olive Oil, Garlic, Lime, Chile Flakes, Salt and Ground Black Pepper to taste.

2. Cut some slices into the chicken but be careful not to cut them all the way through. Coat the Chicken in the mix.

3. Seal the Chicken along with any remaining mix by vacuum sealer of the water displacement method.

Cooking your Honey and Lime Chicken

1. Pre-heat the Sous Vide to 160°F.

2. Cook the Chicken for 2 hours.

Serving

Serve with Salad and Rice.

Spicy Barbecue Chicken Bites

Ingredients

- 500g Boneless Chicken, cubed

- 3 Gloves of Garlic finely chopped and crushed

- 1 Tablespoon of Brown Sugar

- 1 Teaspoon of Paprika

- ½ Teaspoon of Cumin

- ½ Teaspoon of Mustard Powder

- 1 Tablespoon of Olive Oil

- 1 Tablespoon of White Wine Vinegar

- 2 Tablespoons of Golden Syrup

- 3 Tablespoons of Barbecue Sauce

Method

1. Mix all of the ingredients together in a bowl and then mix in the Chicken ensuring all the cubes are evenly covered.

2. Seal the Chicken and any remaining Marinade by vacuum sealer or the water displacement method.

Cooking your Spicy Barbecue Chicken Bites

1. Pre-heat the Sous Vide to 155°F.

2. Cook the Chicken for 2 hours.

3. Remove chicken and place under the grill for 5 minutes or until edges darken.

Serving

Skewer the Chicken pieces and serve hot.

Dry Rub Chicken

Ingredients

- 500g boneless Chicken, cubed.

- 1 Teaspoon of Garlic powder

- 1 Teaspoon of Ginger powder

- 1 Teaspoon of Mustard powder

- ½ Teaspoon Cumin

- ½ Teaspoon Fresh Ground Black Pepper

- Salt to taste

Method

1. Mix the spices together in a bowl.

2. Generously apply an even coating of the Dry Rub mix to the Chicken.

3. Seal the Chicken by vacuum sealer or the water displacement method.

Cooking your Dry Rub Chicken

1. Pre-heat the Sous Vide to 155°F.

2. Cook the Chicken for 2 hours.

3. Remove Chicken and place under the grill for 5 minutes or until edges darken.

Serving

Serve hot with Baked Potato, Salad and Mayo.

Spicy Indian Chicken

Ingredients

- 400g Diced Chicken

- ¼ Teaspoon of Paprika

- ½ Teaspoon of Garam Masala

- ¼ Teaspoon of Chili Powder

- ¼ Teaspoon of Turmeric

- ¼ Teaspoon of Cumin

- 1 teaspoon of Dried Garlic

- ½ Teaspoon of Dried Ginger

Method

1. Mix all of the Spices together in a bowl.

2. Add the Diced Chicken to the Spices and mix well, ensure all the Chicken is fully and evenly covered.

3. Seal the Chicken and any remaining Spice Mix and seal by vacuum sealer or the water displacement method.

Cooking your Spicy Indian Chicken

1. Pre-heat the Sous Vie to 180°F.

2. Cook the Chicken for 2 hours.

3. Remove the Chicken from the Sous Vide.

4. Place the Chicken pieces under a Grill on a high heat for 6 minutes turning midway.

Serving

Serve hot with Pilau Rice

Chicken Teriyaki

Ingredients

- 4 Medium sized Chicken breasts

- 4 Cloves of Garlic finely chopped

- 1 Inch piece of Ginger, grated

- ¼ Teaspoon Chili Powder

- 1 Tablespoon of Brown Sugar

- 3 Tablespoons of Soy Sauce

- 3 Tablespoons of Sake

- 1 Tablespoon of White Wine Vinegar

- ½ Cup of Rice Wine

- Salt and Ground Black Pepper to taste

- Cornflour

- Sesame Oil

Method

1. Mix the Garlic, Ginger, Chili Powder, Brown Sugar, Soy Sauce, Sake, White Wine Vinegar, Rice Wine and a little Salt and Ground Black Pepper to taste.

2. Seal the Marinade and the Chicken by vacuum sealer or the water displacement method.

Cooking your Chicken Teriyaki

1. Pre-heat the Sous Vide to 146°F.

2. Cook the Chicken for 60 minutes.

3. Put some Sesame Oil in a Frying pan on a medium heat.

4. Remove the Chicken from the Sous Vide and place in the Frying Pan. Pour the Marinade in a separate bowl.

5. Cook the Chicken for 4 minutes turning midway.

6. While the Chicken cooks mix some Cornflour into the Marinade 1 teaspoon at a time until the Marinade begins to thicken. This is our Teriyaki Sauce.

Serving

Serve the Chicken atop a bed of White Rice with a drizzle of the Teriyaki sauce and steamed Vegetables.

World Class Chicken Stock

Ingredients

- Bones of 1 Chicken or 6 Chicken Quarters

- 1 Cup of Carrots, diced

- ½ White Onion finely chopped

- 2 Teaspoons of whole Black Peppercorns

- 8 Cups of Water

- ¼ Teaspoon of Salt

- Olive Oil

Method & Cooking your World Class Chicken Stock

1. Pre-heat the oven to 400°F.

2. Mix the Chicken Bones, Onion, Carrots and Olive Oil in a bowl and empty the mix on to an Oven Tray.

3. Pre-heat the Sous Vide to 180°F.

4. Cook the Chicken Bone Mix in the Oven for 20 minutes.

5. Place the Chicken Bone Mix along with any accumulated juices into a Sous Vide bag and seal by the water displacement method.

6. Cook the Chicken Stock for 12-16 hours.

7. Remove the Chicken Stock and strain the liquid discarding any remaining solids.

When refrigerated the Chicken Stock will last 2-3 weeks.

Classic Chicken Quarter

Ingredients

- 2-4 Chicken Quarters

- Salt and Ground Black Pepper to taste

- Olive Oil

Method

1. Season the Chicken Quarters with Salt and a little Ground Black Pepper to taste.

2. Seal the Chicken Quarters by vacuum sealer or the water displacement method.

Cooking your Classic Chicken Quarter

1. Pre-heat the Sous Vide to 164°F.

2. Cook the Chicken Quarters for 90 minutes.

3. Warm some Olive Oil in a Frying Pan on a medium-high heat.

4. Remove the Chicken Quarters from the Sous Vide and pat dry with kitchen towel.

5. Sear the Chicken Quarters Skin down for 1 ½ minutes before serving.

Serving

Serve hot with Bake Potato and Salad.

Whole Chicken

Ingredients

- 1 Whole Chicken

- 1 Litre Chicken Stock

- 1 Cup of chopped Carrot

- 1 Cup of Chopped Onion

- 3 Sprigs of Rosemary

- 3 Sprigs of Thyme

- ½ Teaspoon of Salt

- 1 Teaspoon of Ground Black Pepper

Method

1. Seal all of the ingredients in a Sous Vide bag by the water displacement method.

Cooking your Whole Chicken

1. Pre-heat the Sous Vide to 150°F.

2. Cook the Whole Chicken for 6 hours.

3. Pre-heat the oven to 300°F.

4. Remove the Whole Chicken from the Sous Vide, drain any excess liquid and pat the Whole Chicken dry with kitchen towel.

5. Place the Whole Chicken in the oven for 20 minutes or until the skin is golden brown.

Serving

Serve hot with Mixed Vegetables, Roasted Potatoes and Gravy.

Sous Vide Egg Yolks

Ingredients

- 4-6 Egg Yolks

- 4-6 Slices of Bread

- Salt and Ground Black Pepper

Method

1. Individually seal the Egg Yolks by vacuum sealer or the water displacement method.

Cooking your Sous Vide Egg Yolk

1. Pre-heat the Sous Vide to 143°F.

2. Cook the Egg Yolks for 50-55 minutes.

3. Toast the Bread.

Serving

Serve immediately 'Yolks on Toast' with a little Salt and Ground Black Pepper to taste.

Perfect 'Boiled' Eggs

Ingredients

- 4-6 Eggs

Cooking your Perfect 'Boiled' Eggs

1. Pre-heat the Sous Vide to 174°F.

2. Carefully place the Eggs directly into the Sous Vide and cook for 1 hour.

Serving

Serve alone as a snack or with Salad.

Sous Vide Scrambled Eggs

Ingredients

- 4-6 Eggs

- 2 Tablespoons of Milk

- 2 Teaspoons of Butter

- Salt and Ground Black Pepper to taste

Method

1. Mix all of the Ingredients in a bowl and then separate into 2 Sous Vide bags.

2. Seal by the water displacement method.

Cooking your Sous Vide Scrambled Eggs

1. Pre-heat the Sous Vide to 165°F.

2. Cook the Scrambled Eggs for 15 minutes.

Serving

Serve on Toast for a perfect breakfast

Sous Vide Duck Breasts

Ingredients

- 2-4 Duck Breasts

- 1 Small Orange in Segments

- Salt and Ground Pepper to taste

- Olive Oil

Method

1. Season the Duck Breasts with Salt and Ground Pepper to taste.

Cooking your Sous Vide duck Breasts

1. Pre-heat the Sous Vide to 140°F.

2. Warm a little Olive Oil in a Pan and sear the Duck Breasts skin down on a high heat for 3 minutes.

3. Seal the Duck Breasts and Orange Segments by vacuum sealer or the water displacement method.

4. Cook the Duck Breasts and Orange Segments for 2 hours.

5. Sear the Duck Breasts skin side down for a further 2 minutes.

Serving

Serve Duck Breast atop White Rice and steamed Vegetables with a drizzle of the orange juice from the Sous Vide.

FISH DISHES

Sous Vide Scallops

Ingredients

- 8-10 Fresh Scallops

- 1 Tablespoon of Lemon Juice

- Salt and Ground Black Pepper to taste

- 1 Table spoon of Olive Oil

- 1 Clove of Garlic, chopped

- Olive Oil

Method

1. Seal the Scallops, 1 tablespoon of Lemon Juice and a little Salt and Ground Black Pepper to taste by vacuum sealer or the water displacement method.

Cooking your Sous Vide Scallops

1. Pre-heat the Sous Vide to 130°F.

2. Cook the Scallops for 30 minutes.

3. Warm some Olive Oil and the Garlic in a Frying Pan over a medium heat.

4. Remove the Scallops from the Sous Vide and place the Frying Pan for 2 minutes or until golden, turning midway.

Serving

Serve hot with fresh Salad.

Lemon and Herb Cod

Ingredients

- 2-4 Cod Loin fillets

- 1 Small handful of chopped Basil leaves

- 1 ½ Teaspoons of Italian Mixed Herbs

- 1 Tablespoon of Lemon juice

- 1 Tablespoon of Lime juice

- 2 Tablespoons of Olive Oil

- Salt and Ground Black Pepper to taste

Method

1. Mix all of the ingredients and fully coat the Cod Loins ensuring they're evenly covered.

2. Seal the Cod Loins along with any remaining mix.

Cooking your Lemon and Herb Cod

1. Pre-heat the Sous Vide to 131°F.

2. Cook the Cod Loins for 30 minutes.

Serving

Serve with Salad.

Sous Vide Soy Sauce Cod with Apple

Ingredients

- 4 Cod Fillets

- 1 Clove of Garlic finely chopped

- ½ Teaspoon of Ground Fennel Seeds

- ½ Teaspoon of Dried Dill

- 2 Tablespoons of Soy Sauce

- 2 Tablespoons of Sesame Oil

- Salt and Ground Black Pepper to taste

- 4 Sprigs of Fresh Dill finely chopped

- 1 Fennel Bulb sliced

- 1 Apple, sliced.

Method

1. Mix the Garlic, Ground Fennel Seeds, Dried Dill, Soy Sauce, 1 tablespoon of Sesame Oil.

2. Season the Cod with Salt and Ground Black Pepper and seal by vacuum sealer or the water displacement method.

Garnish

1. In a separate bowl mix the sliced Apple, Fennel, chopped Dill, 1 tablespoon of Sesame Oil and a little Salt and ground Black Pepper to taste.

Cooking your Sous Vide Soy Sauce Cod with Apple

1. Pre-heat the Sous Vide to 130°F.

2. Cook the Cod Fillets for 35 minutes.

Serving

Serve hot with the sliced Apple, Fennel and Dill garnish.

Garlic, Chili and Ginger Cod Loin

Ingredients

- 2-4 Cod Loin fillets

- 3 Cloves of Garlic finely chopped

- 1 Inch piece of Ginger, grated

- ½ Teaspoon of Dried Chili flakes

- 1 Tablespoon of Lemon juice

- 2 Tablespoons of Olive Oil

- Salt and Ground Black Pepper to taste

Method

1. Mix all of the ingredients and fully coat the Cod Loins ensuring they are evenly covered.

2. Seal the Cod Loins along with any remaining mix.

Cooking your Garlic, Chili and Ginger Cod Loin

1. Pre-heat the Sous Vide to 131°F.

2. Cook the Cod Loins for 30 minutes.

Serving

Serve with Salad and White Rice.

Sous Vide Thai Style Salmon

Ingredients

- 2-4 Boneless Salmon Fillets

- 1 Inch piece of Ginger, grated

- 2 Lemongrass stalks sliced lengthways

- 1 White Onion finely chopped

- 2 Red Chilies seeded and chopped

- 1 Teaspoon of Coriander

- 1 Teaspoon of Crushed Peppercorns

- 2 Kaffir Lime Leaves, chopped

- 1 Tablespoon Sesame Oil

- Salt and Ground Pepper to taste

Method

1. In a bowl, mix the Ginger, Lemongrass Stalks, Onion, Chillies, Coriander, Crushed Peppercorns, Lime Leaves, Sesame Oil and a little Salt and Ground Black Pepper to taste.

2. Place the Salmon in the mix, fully cover and seal by vacuum sealer or water displacement method.

Cooking your Sous Vide Thai Style Salmon

1. Pre-heat the Sous Vide to 115°F.

2. Cook the Salmon for 30 minutes.

Serving

Serve with Rice or Fries with Salad.

Lemon, Rosemary and Thyme Salmon Steaks

Ingredients

- 2-4 Salmon Steaks

- 2 Teaspoons of Dried Rosemary

- 2 Teaspoons of Dried Thyme

- 2 Garlic Cloves finely chopped

- 2 Tablespoons of Olive Oil

- 2 Tablespoons of Fresh Lemon Juice

- ¼ Teaspoon Fresh Ground Pepper

- Salt to taste

Method

1. Mix together the Rosemary, Thyme, 1 clove of Garlic, Olive Oil, Lemon juice, Ground Pepper and a little Salt to taste.

Cooking your Lemon, Rosemary and Thyme Salmon Steaks

1. Pre-heat the Sous Vide to 120°F.

2. Cook the Salmon Steaks for 30 minutes.

3. Remove the Salmon Steaks from the Sous Vide and heat some Olive Oil in a pan and add 1 clove of finely chopped Garlic.

4. Cook on a medium heat for 1 ½ minutes.

5. Add the Salmon Steaks to the Pan and cook for 1 minute on either side.

Serving

Serve hot with a squeeze of Lemon.

Basil, Garlic and Ginger Salmon

Ingredients

- 4-6 Salmon Fillets

- 2 Cloves of Garlic finely chopped

- 1 Inch Piece of Ginger, grated

- 1 Handful of Fresh Basil Leaves, chopped

- 1 Shallot, chopped

- 2 Tablespoons of Lemon Juice

- Salt and Ground Black Pepper to taste

- 1 Tablespoon of Olive Oil

- 1 Tablespoon of Butter

Method

1. Seal all of the ingredients by vacuum sealer or the water displacement method.

Cooking your Basil, Garlic and Ginger Salmon

1. Pre-heat the Sous Vide to 124°F.

2. Cook the Salmon Fillets for 30 minutes.

3. Melt the Butter in a Pan over a medium heat.

4. Remove the Salmon Fillets from the Sous Vide and place Skin down in the Pan with the melted butter.

5. Cook the Salmon for 2 minutes.

Serving

Serve hot with Green Salad and a squeeze of Lemon Juice.

Zahtar Salmon

Ingredients

- 2 Salmon Fillets

- 1 ½ Teaspoons of Zahtar Spice

- 1 Clove of Garlic finely chopped

- 1 Teaspoon of Dried Coriander

- 1 Tablespoon of Lemon Juice

- Salt and Ground Black Pepper to taste

- Olive Oil

Method

1. Mix the Zahtar, Coriander, Lemon Juice and a little Salt and Ground Black Pepper to taste.

2. Coat the Salmon Fillets in the mix and seal along with the Garlic and any leftover mix by vacuum sealer or the water displacement method.

Cooking your Zahtar Salmon

1. Pre-heat the Sous Vide to 130°F.

2. Cook the Salmon for 30 minutes.

3. Warm some Olive Oil in a Frying Pan on a medium-high heat.

4. Remove the Salmon and place Skin down in the Frying Pan, sear for 2 minutes before serving.

Serving

Serve hot on a bed of Rice with a squeeze of Lemon Juice.

Sous Vide Seared Mackerel with Coriander and Lime

Ingredients

- 4 Mackerel Fillets, deboned

- 2 Red Chilies seeded and finely chopped

- 1 Inch piece of Ginger, grated

- 2 Clove of Garlic finely grated

- ½ Teaspoon of Dried Coriander

- 1 Handful of Spring Onions chopped

- 1 Tablespoon of fresh Lime Juice

- Salt and Ground Black Pepper to taste

Method

1. Mix the Chilies, Ginger, Garlic, Coriander, Spring Onions, Lime Juice and a little Salt and Pepper to taste.

2. Coat the Mackerel in the mix and seal along with any leftover marinade by vacuum sealer or the water displacement method.

Cooking your Sous Vide Seared Mackerel with Coriander and Lime

1. Pre-heat the Sous Vide to 120°F.

2. Cook the Mackerel for 25 minutes.

3. Remove the Mackerel from the Sous Vide and heat some Olive Oil in a pan over a high heat for 30 seconds.

4. Add the Mackerel to the Pan Skin side down and cook for 1½ minutes.

Serve

Serve hot with White Rice and Salad.

Lemon and Garlic Chili Prawns

Ingredients

- 500g Prawns peeled and cleaned

- 2 Cloves of Garlic finely chopped

- 1 Pinch of Chili Flakes

- 2 Tablespoon of Lemon Juice

- Salt and Ground Black Pepper to taste

Method

1. Mix together the Prawns, Garlic, Chili Flakes, Lemon Juice and a little Salt and Pepper to taste.

2. Seal the Prawns along with any remaining marinade by vacuum sealer or the water displacement method.

Cooking your Lemon and Garlic Chili Prawns

1. Pre-heat the Sous Vide to 135°F.

2. Cook the Lemon and Garlic Chili Prawns for 30 minutes.

Serving

Serve hot with chopped Spring Onion as a starter or with Rice as a main.

Lemon and Lime Seabass

Ingredients

- 4-6 Seabass fillets, deboned

- 2 Cloves of Garlic finely chopped

- 2 Tablespoons of Lemon Juice

- 2 Tablespoons of Lime Juice

- ¼ Teaspoon of Dried Basil

- ¼ Teaspoon of Dried Oregano

- ¼ Teaspoon of Thyme

- Salt and Ground Black Pepper to taste

Method

1. Mix the Herbs, Garlic, Lemon and Lime in a bowl.

2. Place the Seabass Fillets in the mix ensuring the Seabass Fillets are fully coated.

3. Seal the Seabass Fillets along with any remaining Marinade by vacuum sealer or the water displacement method.

Cooking you Lemon and Lime Seabass

1. Pre-heat the Sous Vide to 150°F.

2. Cook the Lemon and Lime Seabass for 30.

3. Remove the Seabass fillets from the Sous Vide and place Skin down in a pan on a medium-high heat for 2 minutes or until the skin begins to crisp.

Serving

Serve hot with Rice or Salad.

Sous Vide Tomato and Herb Seabass

Ingredients

- 4 Seabass Fillets

- 1 Packet of Sun-dried Tomatoes, chopped

- 1 Handful of Cherry Tomatoes, chopped

- ½ Teaspoon of Dried Basil

- 1 Teaspoon of Mixed Herbs

- 1 Tablespoon Tomato Puree

- 2 Cloves of Garlic finely chopped

- ½ White Onion finely chopped

- Salt and Ground Black Pepper to taste

Method

1. Mix the Sun-Dried Tomatoes, Cherry Tomatoes and crush them with the back of a spoon.

2. Add the Mixed Herbs, Basil, Tomato Puree, Garlic, Onion, Salt and Ground Black Pepper.

3. Coat the Seabass in the Tomato and Herb Marinade and seal along with some Marinade mix by vacuum sealer or the water displacement method.

Cooking your Tomato and Herb Seabass

1. Pre-heat the Sous Vide to 150°F.

2. Cook the Seabass fillets for 30 minutes.

Serving

Serve hot with Rice or Salad and Pesto with a drizzle of the leftover Tomato and Herb Sauce Marinade.

Simple Chili Seabass

Ingredients

- 4 Seabass Fillets

- Salt and Ground Black Pepper to taste

- 1 Teaspoon of Chili Flakes

- Olive Oil

Method

1. Season the Seabass Fillets with the Chili Flakes, Salt and Ground Black Pepper to taste.

2. Seal the Seabass Fillets by vacuum sealer of the water displacement method.

Cooking your Simple Chili Seabass

1. Pre-heat the Sous Vide to 136°F.

2. Cook the Chili Seabass for 30 minutes.

3. Warm some Olive Oil in a Frying Pan over a medium-high heat.

4. Remove the Seabass from the Sous Vide and place Skin down in the Frying Pan.

5. Cook the Seabass for 2-4 minutes.

Serving

Serve hot with White Rice, Salad and a squeeze of Lemon Juice.

Lobster and Scampi Sauce

Ingredients

- 400g Lobster meat cut into even sized large chunks

- 3 Cloves of Garlic finely chopped

- 1 Teaspoon of Italian Mixed Herbs

- 1 Teaspoon of Dijon Mustard

- 1 Tablespoon of Fresh Parsley finely chopped

- 2 Tablespoons of Lemon Juice

- 1 ½ Cups of White Wine

- ½ Cup of unsalted Butter

- ½ Cup Parmesan Cheese

- Olive Oil

- Salt and Ground Black Pepper to taste

Method

1. Seal the Lobster and 2 teaspoons of Butter along with a little Salt and Ground Black Pepper to taste. Do this by vacuum sealer or the water displacement method.

Cooking your Scampi Sauce

1. Put a small saucepan on medium heat and add a dash of Olive Oil.

2. Add the Garlic and cook for 1-2 minutes before mixing in the White Wine, Lemon Juice and Dijon Mustard, cook until the wine has reduced by half.

3. Add the Italian Mixed Herbs and Butter and reduce to a low heat.

4. Mix in the chopped Parsley and a little Salt and Ground Black Pepper to taste.

5. Before serving add a sprinkling of Parmesan Cheese.

Cooking your Lobster

1. Pre-heat the Sous Vide to 135°F.

2. Cook the Lobster for 45 minutes.

Serving

Serve hot with a drizzle of Scampi Sauce and Parmesan Cheese.

Sous Vide Tuna Steaks

Ingredients

- 2-4 Tuna Steaks

- ¼ Teaspoon of Dried Dill

- ¼ Teaspoon of Dried Thyme

- ½ Cup of Chopped Shallots

- Salt and Ground Black Pepper to taste

- 2 Tablespoons of Black and White Sesame Seeds

- Olive Oil

Method

1. Season the Tuna Steaks with Salt and Ground Black Pepper.

2. Seal the Tuna Steaks, Dried Dill, Dried Thyme and Shallots by vacuum sealer or the water displacement method.

Cooking your Sous Vide Tuna Steaks

1. Pre-heat the Sous Vide to 140°F.

2. Cook the Tuna Steaks for 45 minutes.

3. Remove the Tuna Steaks from the Sous Vide and generously coat each side of the Tuna with Black and White Sesame Seeds and a little Ground Black Pepper.

4. Heat some Olive Oil in a Frying Pan on a medium-high heat.

5. Cook the Tuna Steaks for 3 minutes turning midway.

Serving

Serve immediately with steamed Vegetables and White Rice.

Sesame and Ginger Tuna Steaks

Ingredients

- 2 Tuna Steaks

- 2 Cloves of Garlic finely chopped

- 1 Inch piece of Ginger, grated

- 2 Tablespoon of Soy Sauce

- ¼ Cup of Salt

- 1 Tablespoon of Sugar

- Salt and Ground Black Pepper to taste

- ¼ Cup of Toasted Sesame Seeds

- Sesame Oil

Method

1. Mix the Water, ¼ cup of Salt and Sugar in a large bowl.

2. Add the Tuna Steaks to the Water, Sugar and Salt mix (brine), cover and refrigerate for 30 minutes.

3. Remove the Tuna steaks from the Brine and pat dry using kitchen towel.

4. Seal the Tuna steaks, Garlic, Ginger and a little Salt and Ground Black Pepper to taste by vacuum sealer or the water displacement method.

Cooking your Sesame and Ginger Tuna Steaks

1. Pre-heat the Sous Vide to 115°F.

2. Cook the Tuna Steaks for 30 minutes.

3. Remove the Tune Steaks from the Sous Vide, pat dry using kitchen towel.

4. Warm some Sesame Oil in a Frying Pan on a medium heat.

5. Coat the Tuna Steaks in the Sesame Seeds.

6. Place the Tune Steaks in the Frying Pan and cook for 3 minutes, turning midway.

Serving

Serve hot or cold with White Rice and Salad.

Sous Vide Trout

Ingredients

- 2-4 Trout Fillets

- 1 Handful of chopped Parsley

- 2 Tablespoons of Lemon Juice

- Salt and Ground Black Pepper

- Olive Oil

Method

1. Seal the Trout, Lemon Juice and Parsley by vacuum sealer or the water displacement method.

Cooking your Sous Vide Trout

1. Pre-heat the Sous Vide to 130°F.

2. Cook the Trout for 30 minutes.

3. Warm some Olive Oil in a Frying Pan over a medium-high heat.

4. Remove the Trout from the Sous Vide.

5. Sear the Trout Skin down for 2 minutes or until the skin begins to crisp.

Serving

Serve hot with Green Beans or Salad.

LAMB DISHES

Lebanese Lamb

Ingredients

- 400g Minced Lamb
- 2 Teaspoons of Shawarma Seasoning
- 3 Cloves of Garlic finely chopped
- Salt and Ground Black Pepper
- Olive Oil

Method

1. Evenly mix the Shawarma Seasoning, Garlic, and a little Salt and Ground Black Pepper to taste into the minced lamb.
2. Seal the Lamb by vacuum sealer or the water displacement method.

Cooking your Lebanese Lamb

1. Pre-heat the Sous Vide to 140°F.
2. Cook the Lamb for 2 hours.
3. Warm some Olive Oil in a Frying Pan over a medium heat.
4. Remove the Lamb from the Sous Vide and drain any excess liquids.
5. Fry the Lamb for 4 minutes.

Serving

Serve with Cumin Roasted Carrots, Couscous and a dollop of Home Made Yoghurt.

Lamb and Charred Pepper Teriyaki Skewers

Ingredients

- 400g Diced Lamb

- 2 Red Peppers cut into chunks

- 1 Yellow Peppers cut into chunks

- 4 Cloves of Garlic finely chopped

- 1 Inch piece of Ginger, grated

- ¼ Teaspoon Chili Powder

- 1 Tablespoon of Brown Sugar

- 3 Tablespoons of Soy Sauce

- 3 Tablespoons of Sake

- 1 Tablespoon of White Wine Vinegar

- ½ Cup of Rice Wine

- Salt and Ground Black Pepper to taste

- Cornflour

- Sesame Oil

- Skewers

Method

1. Mix the Garlic, Ginger, Chili Powder, Brown Sugar, Soy Sauce, Sake, White Wine Vinegar, Rice wine and a little Salt and Ground Black Pepper to taste.

2. Seal the Marinade and the Lamb by vacuum sealer or the water displacement method.

Cooking your Lamb and Charred Pepper Teriyaki Skewers

1. Pre-heat the Sous Vide to 140°F.

2. Cook the Lamb for 90 minutes.

3. Put some Sesame Oil in a Frying pan on a medium heat.

4. Remove the Lamb from the Sous Vide and place in the Frying Pan. Pour the Marinade in a separate bowl.

5. Place the Peppers on the Grill under a high heat and cook for 5 minutes or until the skin begins to char.

6. Cook the Lamb for 4 minutes turning midway.

7. While the Lamb cooks mix some Cornflour into the Marinade 1 teaspoon at a time until the Marinade begins to thicken. This is our Teriyaki Sauce.

Serving

Skewer the Lamb along with the Peppers and top with a drizzle of the Teriyaki sauce and some white rice.

Lamb Ribs

Ingredients

- 2 Racks of Lamb Ribs

- 3 Cloves of Garlic finely chopped

- 2 Teaspoon of Dried Coriander

- 2 Teaspoon of Dried Cumin

- 3 Teaspoons of Brown Sugar

- 1 Teaspoon Chili Flakes

- 1 Teaspoon of Salt

- 1 Teaspoon of Ground Black Pepper

- Olive Oil

Method

1. Mix all of the ingredients together, split the mix between 2 bowls and use one to fully coat the Lamb Ribs.

2. Seal the Lamb Ribs and any remaining Marinade by vacuum sealer or the water displacement method.

Cooking your Lamb Ribs

1. Pre-heat the Sous Vide to 138°F.

2. Cook the Lamb Ribs for 12 hours or overnight.

3. Warm some Olive Oil over in a Frying Pan over a medium heat.

4. Remove the Lamb Ribs from the Sous Vide and coat again the remaining Marinade.

5. Place the Lamb Ribs in the Frying Pan and cook for 3 minutes turning midway.

Serving

Serve hot as the perfect appetiser.

Minted Lamb Chops

Ingredients

- 4 Lamb Chops

- 1 Handful of chopped Mint Leaves

- 4 Sprigs of Fresh Thyme

- Salt and Ground Black Pepper to taste

- Olive Oil

Method

1. Season the Lamb Chops with a little Salt and Pepper to taste.

2. Seal the Lamb, Mint and Thyme by vacuum sealer or the water displacement method.

Cooking your Minted Lamb Chops

1. Pre-heat the Sous Vide to 140°F.

2. Cook the Lamb Chops for 2 hours.

3. Warm some Olive Oil in a Frying Pan or Griddle over a medium-high heat.

4. Place the Lamb in the Frying Pan or Griddle and cook for 4 minutes or until the Lamb Chops begin to brown, turn midway.

Serving

Serve with Boiled Potatoes, Mixed Vegetables and Gravy.

Spicy Indian Lamb

Ingredients

- 400g Diced Lamb

- ¼ Teaspoon of Paprika

- ½ Teaspoon of Garam Masala

- ¼ Teaspoon of Chili Powder

- ¼ Teaspoon of Turmeric

- ¼ Teaspoon of Cumin

- 1 Teaspoon of Dried Garlic

- ½ Teaspoon of Dried Ginger

Method

1. Mix all of the Spices together in a bowl.

2. Add the Diced Lamb to the Spices and mix well, ensure all the Lamb is fully and evenly covered.

3. Seal the Lamb and any remaining Spice Mix and seal by vacuum sealer or the water displacement method.

Cooking your Spicy Indian Lamb

1. Pre-heat the Sous Vie to 140°F.

2. Cook the Lamb for 2 hours.

3. Remove the Lamb from the Sous Vide.

4. Place the Lamb Pieces under a Grill on a high heat for 6 minutes turning midway.

Serving

Serve hot with Pilau Rice.

Garlic and Rosemary Leg of Lamb

Ingredients

- 1 Large boneless Leg of Lamb

- 2 Cloves of Garlic finely chopped

- 1 Red Onion, chopped

- 4 Sprigs of Rosemary

- 2 Sprigs of Thyme

- Salt and Ground Black Pepper to taste

- ½ Cup of Red wine

- 2 Tablespoons of Flour

- 1 Tablespoon of Butter

- ¼ Cup of Beef Stock

- 1 Tablespoon of Orange Juice

Method

1. Mix together the Garlic, Rosemary, Thyme, Onion and a little Salt and Ground Black Pepper to taste.

2. Rub the Herb, Garlic and Onion mix into the Leg of Lamb and seal by vacuum sealer or the water displacement method.

Cooking your Garlic and Rosemary Leg of Lamb

1. Pre-heat the Sous Vide to 134°F.

2. Cook the Leg of Lamb for 8 hours to overnight.

3. Pre-heat the Oven to 300°F.

4. Remove the Lamb from the sous Vide, pat dry with kitchen towel and pour the cooking liquids a separate bowl.

5. Place on the middle shelf of the Oven and cook the Lamb for 14-20 minutes or until brown.

6. Whilst the lamb is cooking melt the butter in a Saucepan over a medium heat.

7. When the Butter has melted add the Flour, Red Wine, Beef stock, Orange Juice and the leftover cooking juices.

8. Stir the Sauce until reduced by half.

Serving

Serve hot with Roasted Potatoes, Mixed Vegetables and a drizzle of the cooking sauce.

Oriental Roast Lamb Chops

Ingredients

- 4-6 Lamb Chops

- 1 Clove of Garlic finely chopped

- 1 ½ Inch piece of Ginger, grated

- 1 Tablespoon of Soy Sauce

- 2 Stalks of Lemongrass sliced lengthways

- 1 ½ Half Teaspoons of Coriander

- 1 Cup of Sesame Seeds

- 1 Tablespoon of Sesame Oil

- 1 Teaspoon of Honey

Method

1. Mix the Soy sauce, Ginger, Garlic, Lemongrass, Coriander, Sesame Oil and Honey in a bowl.

2. Coat the Lamb Chops in the mix, ensure they are evenly coated.

3. Seal the Lamb Chops along with any remaining marinade mix by vacuum sealer or the water displacement method.

Cooking your Roast Lamb

1. Pre-heat the Sous Vide to 138°F.

2. Cook the Lamb Chops for 3-4 hours.

3. Remove the Pork Chops from the Sous Vide and lightly coat them in the Sesame Seeds.

4. Pre-heat the Oven to 300°F.

5. Place the Lamb Chops on a Baking Tray and put in the Oven on the middle shelf and cook for 10-15 minutes.

Serving

Serve with White Rice and Steamed Vegetables.

Moroccan Lamb

Ingredients

- 600g Diced Lamb
- Moroccan Spice Mix
- 2 Tablespoon of Honey
- 1 Pack of Dried Apricots
- Salt and Ground Black Pepper
- Olive Oil

Method

1. Season the Lamb with a little Salt and Ground Black Pepper to taste.
2. Seal all the ingredients by vacuum sealer or the water displacement method.

Cooking your Moroccan Lamb

1. Pre-heat the Sous Vide to 138°F.
2. Cook the Lamb for 2 hours.
3. Heat some Olive Oil in a Frying Pan over a medium heat.
4. Remove the Lamb from the Sous Vide and place the cooking liquid to one side.
5. Sear the Lamb in the Frying Pan for 4 minutes or until brown, turning midway.

Serving

Serve hot with Salad and a drizzle of the cooking sauce.

PORK DISHES

Smokey Pulled Pork

Ingredients

- 350g Pork Shoulder Joint

- 2 Cloves of Garlic finely chopped

- 1 Tablespoon of Liquid Smoke

- Salt and Fresh Ground Black Pepper

- Barbecue Sauce

Method

1. Seal all of the ingredients by vacuum sealer of the water displacement method.

Cooking your Smokey Pulled Pork

1. Pre-heat the Sous Vide to 160°F.

2. Cook the Pork for 26 hours.

3. Shred the Pork using forks and mix with Barbecue Sauce to taste.

Serving

Serve as sliders with Coleslaw.

Honey Roast Ham

Ingredients

- 1kg Pork Joint

- 2 Tablespoons of Honey

- 1 Teaspoon of Mustard

- Salt to taste

Method

1. Soak the Point in Salt Water for 24 hours.

2. Seal the Ham by vacuum sealer or the water displacement method.

Cooking your Honey Roast Ham

1. Pre-heat the Sous Vide to 150°F.

2. Cook the Pork joint for 48 hours.

3. Remove the still sealed Ham from the Sous Vide and Place the bag into some Ice water to cool.

4. When cool mix the Honey and Mustard, score the Ham in a diamond pattern with a sharp knife and generously coat the Ham with the Honey and Mustard mix.

5. Pre-heat the oven to 300°F.

6. Place the Ham on the middle shelf of the Oven and cook for 20 minutes.

Serving

Serve as a centrepiece with roast Mixed Vegetables.

Lemongrass and Garlic Pork Chops

Ingredients

- 2-4 Pork chops on the Bone

- 2 Lemongrass Stalks sliced lengthways

- 4 Cloves of Garlic finely chopped

- 1 Inch piece of Garlic, grated

- 1 Tablespoon of Rice Wine Vinegar

- 1 Tablespoon of Soy Sauce

- 1 Tablespoon of Brown Sugar

- Salt and Ground Black Pepper

- Olive Oil

Method

1. Mix all of the ingredients together then add the Pork Chops ensuring they're fully covered in the Marinade.

2. Seal the Pork Chops and any remaining Marinade by vacuum sealer or the water displacement method.

Cooking your Lemongrass and Garlic Pork Chops

1. Pre-heat the Sous Vide to 144°F.

2. Cook the Pork Chops for 2 hours.

3. Remove the Pork Chops from the Sous Vide, pat dry with a kitchen towel.

4. Warm some Olive Oil in a Frying Pan or Griddle over a medium-high heat.

5. Sear the Pork Chops for 1 minute on either side.

Serving

Serve hot with Mash Potato.

Sous Vide Gammon and Pineapple

Ingredients

- Gammon Steaks

- Pineapples Rings 1 per Gammon Steak

- Salt and Ground Pepper to taste

- ¼ Teaspoon of Cayenne Pepper

Method

1. Season the Gammon Steaks with Cayenne Pepper, Salt and Ground Black Pepper to taste.

2. Seal the Gammon Steaks and Pineapple Rings by vacuum sealer or the water displacement method.

Cooking your Sous Vide Gammon and Pineapple

1. Pre-heat the Sous Vide to 150°F.

2. Cook the Gammon Steaks and Pineapple for 60 minutes.

3. Remove the Gammon from the Sous Vide and put the Pineapple slices to one side.

4. Place the Gammon Steaks on the Grill and cook for 3 minutes or until golden brown, turning midway.

Serving

Place a Pineapple ring on each of the Gammon Steaks and serve hot with Fries or Baked Potato and Salad.

Sous Vide (BLT) Bacon Lettuce and Tomato Sandwiches

Ingredients

- 1 Packet of Bacon of choice

- Fresh Lettuce

- Fresh sliced Tomato

- Slice Bread

Method

1. Seal the Bacon by vacuum sealer or the water displacement method.

Cooking you Sous Vide Bacon

1. Pre-heat the Sous Vide to 145°F.

2. Cook the Bacon for 48 to 72 hours.

3. Remove the Bacon from the Sous Vide and separate the slices.

4. Place on a hot Griddle, Frying Pan or Grill for 3 minutes turning midway or until the Bacon begins to crisp.

5. Remove excess grease with a paper towel.

Serving

Serve in Sandwiches with Lettuce and Tomato.

Sous Vide Sausages

Ingredients

- 8 Sausages

- ½ Cup of Cider

- 1 Onion chopped

Method

1. Seal the Sausages along with the Cider by vacuum sealer or the water displacement method.

Cooking your Sous Vide Sausages

1. Pre-heat the Sous Vide to 155°F.

2. Cook the Sausages for 60 minutes.

3. Remove the Sausages from the Sous Vide and place in a Frying Pan along with a little Olive Oil and the chopped Onions on a medium heat.

4. Cook for 3 minutes or until golden, turning midway.

Serving

Serve with Hotdog Buns, Ketchup and Mustard.

Pork Chops

Ingredients

- 4 Pork Chops
- 1 Teaspoon of Dried Rosemary
- 1 Teaspoon of Dried Thyme
- 1 Teaspoon of Butter
- Salt and Ground Black Pepper to taste
- Olive Oil

Method

1. Season the Pork Chops with the Dried Rosemary, Dried Thyme and a little Salt and Ground Black Pepper to taste.
2. Seal the Pork Chops by vacuum sealer or the water displacement method.

Cooking your Pork Chops

1. Pre-heat the Sous Vide to 136°F.
2. Cook the Pork Chops for 60 minutes.
3. Warm some Olive Oil and the Butter in a Frying Pan on a medium heat.
4. Remove the Pork Chops from the Sous Vide and place them into the Frying Pan.
5. Cook for 4 minutes, turning midway.

Serving

Serve hot with Baked Potato and mixed Vegetables.

Peppered Pork with Chorizo

Ingredients

- 2-4 Pork Medallions

- 1 Packet of Chorizo chopped into cubes.

- 1 Teaspoon of Black Peppercorns

- 2 Cloves of Garlic finely chopped

Method

1. Seal all of the ingredients by vacuum sealer or the water misplacement method.

Cooking your Peppered Pork with Chorizo

1. Pre-heat the Sous Vide to 140°F.

2. Cook the Pork for 2 hours.

Serving

Serve with boiled Potatoes and Salad.

Oriental Pork Medallions

Ingredients

- 4 Pork Medallions

- 1 Clove of Garlic finely chopped

- 1 Inch Piece of Garlic

- 2 Lemongrass Stalks

- 2 Tablespoon of Soy Sauce

- ½ Tablespoon of Dried Coriander

- Salt and Ground Black Pepper to taste

- Sesame Oil

- 1 Tablespoon of Lime Juice

Method

1. Mix all of the ingredients together in a bowl making sure that the Pork Medallions are evenly covered.

2. Seal the Pork Medallions and any remaining mix by vacuum sealer or the water displacement method.

Cooking your Oriental Pork Medallions

1. Pre-heat the Sous Vide to 150°F.

2. Cook the Oriental Pork Medallions for 4-6 hours.

3. Warm some Sesame Oil in a Frying Pan on a medium-high heat.

4. Remove the Pork Medallions from the Sous Vide and place in the Frying Pan.

5. Cook the Pork Medallions for 4 minutes or until brown, turning midway.

Serving

Serve hot with White Rice, Salad and a drizzle of the cooking Marinade.

Sweet and Sticky Pork Belly

Ingredients

- 800g Pork Belly cut into strips

- Salt and Ground Black Pepper

- ¼ Teaspoon of Chili Flakes

- 2 Tablespoons of Brown Sugar

- 1 Clove of Garlic finely chopped

- 1 Tablespoon of Lime Juice

- 1 Tablespoon of Sesame Oil

- ¼ Cup Char Sui Sauce

Method

1. Mix the Chili Flakes, Brown Sugar, Sesame Oil, Garlic, Lime Juice and a little salt and Pepper to taste in a bowl.

2. Coat the Pork Belly Strips in the mix and seal along with any remaining mix by vacuum sealer or the water displacement method.

Cooking your Sweet and Sticky Pork Belly

1. Pre-heat the Sous Vide to 156°F.

2. Cook the Pork Belly for 18-24 hours.

3. Pre-heat the Oven to 300°F.

4. Remove the Pork Belly from the Sous Vide place on a Baking Tray.

5. Give both sides of the Pork Belly Strips a generous coating of the Char Sui Sauce and place on the middle shelf in the Oven.

6. Cook the Pork Belly Strips for 8-10 minutes.

7. Apply a second coat of the Char Sui Sauce and cook for a further 5 minutes.

Serving

Serve immediately with Salad.

Sous Vide Spicy Fried Spam

Ingredients

- 1 Tin of Spam horizontally sliced into 1cm slices

- ½ Teaspoon of Ground Black Pepper

- ½ Teaspoon of medium heat Chili Flakes

- ¼ Teaspoon of Paprika

- ¼ Teaspoon of Cumin

- ½ Cup Olive Oil

Method

1. Mix the Chili Flakes, Cumin, Ground Black Pepper and Paprika in a bowl.

2. Lightly coat the Spam slices with the Chili Flakes, Cumin, Paprika and Ground Black Pepper mix.

3. Seal the Spam slices by vacuum sealer or the water displacement method.

Cooking your Sous Vide Fried Spam

1. Pre-heat the Sous Vide to 140°F.

2. Cook the Spam Slices for 40-60 minutes.

3. Warm ½ Cup of Olive Oil in a Pan on a medium-high heat.

4. Remove the Spam Slices from the Sous Vide and place into the Pan with the Olive Oil.

5. Fry the Spam Slices for 6 minutes or until golden, turning midway.

Serving

Serve with Fries/Chips and Salad.

VEGETABLE DISHES AND SIDES

Buttery Garlic Mash Potato

Ingredients

- 800g Maris Piper Potatoes, peeled and quartered

- ¼ Cup of Butter

- 1 Teaspoon of Garlic Paste

Methods

1. Seal all of the ingredients by vacuum sealer or the water displacement method.

Cooking your Buttery Garlic Mash Potato

1. Pre-heat the Sous Vide to 194°F.

2. Cook the Potatoes for 36-40 minutes.

3. Remove potatoes from the Sous Vide and mash.

Serving

A perfect side at Barbecues.

Sous Vide Roast Potatoes

Ingredients

- 500g Maris Piper Potatoes, peeled and halved

- 2 Cloves of Garlic finely chopped

- 1 Teaspoon of dried Rosemary

- 2 Tablespoons of Olive Oil

- Salt and Ground Black Pepper to taste

Method

1. Seal all of the ingredients by vacuum sealer or the water displacement method.

Cooking your Sous Vide Roast Potatoes

1. Pre-heat the Sous Vide to 130°F.

2. Cook the Potatoes for 30 minutes.

3. Pre-heat the Oven to 300°F.

4. Remove the Potatoes from the Sous Vide and place in a Baking Try on the middle shelf of the Oven.

5. Cook the Potatoes for 30 minutes or until golden, turning midway.

Serving

Serve hot with Beef, Chicken or Pork.

Sous Vide Mint Potatoes

Ingredients

- 500g Maris Piper Potatoes, peeled and quartered

- 1 Tablespoon of Butter

- 1 Handful of Fresh Mint Leaves, chopped

- Salt to taste

Method

1. Seal the Potatoes, Butter, Mint Leaves and a little Salt to taste by vacuum sealer or the water displacement method.

Cooking your Sous Vide Mint Potatoes

1. Pre-heat the Sous Vide to 190°F.

2. Cook the Potatoes for 30 minutes.

Serving

Serve hot with Salad or Steak and Salad.

Sous Vide Corn on the Cob

Ingredients

- 4 Corn Cobs

- 2 Tablespoon of Butter

- Salt and Ground Black Pepper (optional) to taste

Method

1. Season the Corns Cobs with a little salt.

2. Seal the Corn Cobs and Butter by vacuum sealer or the water displacement method.

Cooking your Sous Vide Corn on the Cob

1. Pre-heat the Sous Vide for 184°F.

2. Cook for 50 minutes.

Serving

Serve hot with Salt.

Cumin Roasted Carrots

Ingredients

- 350g Carrots, chopped julienne

- 1 Teaspoon of Cumin

- Salt and Ground Black Pepper to taste

Method

1. Mix the Cumin with a little Salt and Ground Pepper and generously coat the Carrots.

2. Seal the Carrots by vacuum sealer or the water displacement method.

Cooking your Cumin Roasted Carrots

1. Pre-heat the Sous Vide to 185°F.

2. Cook the Carrots for 45 minutes.

3. Pre-heat the oven to 280°F.

4. Remove the Carrots from the Sous Vide, place on the middle shelf of the oven and cook for 15 minutes.

Serving

Serve hot with Salmon or Pork.

Green Beans and Apricots

Ingredients

- 300g Green Beans, trimmed

- 1 Packet of Dried Apricots chopped

- 1 Tablespoon of butter

- Salt to taste

Method

1. Simple seal all of the ingredients by vacuum sealer of the water displacement method.

Cooking Your Green Beans and Apricots

1. Pre-heat the Sous Vide to 185°F.

2. Cook the Green Beans for 60 minutes.

Serving

Serve hot with Beef or Pork Dishes.

Sous Vide Asparagus

Ingredients

- 300g Asparagus

- ½ Tablespoon of Butter

- Salt and Ground Black Pepper to taste

Method

1. Simple seal all of the ingredients by vacuum sealer of the water displacement method.

Cooking your Sous Vide Asparagus

1. Pre-heat the Sous Vide to 180°F.

2. Cook the Asparagus for 60 minutes.

Serving

Serve hot with Steak or Salmon.

Sous Vide Beets

Ingredients

- 300g Beetroot, peeled and sliced
- 1 Tablespoon of Balsamic Vinegar
- 1 Tablespoon of Lemon Juice
- ½ Cup of Orange Juice
- 1 Tablespoon of Honey
- ¼ Teaspoon Black Peppercorns
- Salt to taste

Method

1. Mix all of the ingredients in a large bowl and seal by the water displacement method.

Cooking your Sous Vide Beets

1. Pre-heat the Sous Vide to 180°F.
2. Cook the Beets for 90 minutes.
3. Remove the Beets from the Sous Vide and pour only the liquid into a Saucepan and place on a medium heat, stirring continuously until the liquid has reduced by half.
4. Once the liquid has reduced, add the Beets to the liquid, stir and serve.

Serving

Serve hot as an appetiser.

Tomato Confit

Ingredients

- 1 Packet of Cherry Tomatoes on the vine

- Salt and Ground Black Pepper to taste

- 2 Sprigs of Rosemary

- 2 Sprigs of Thyme

- 1 Teaspoon of Sugar

- 2 Tablespoons Balsamic Vinegar

- 1 Tablespoon Olive Oil

Method

1. Cut a small X into the top of each of the Tomatoes and place them into boiling water for 1 minute or until the skins begins to crinkle and peel.

2. Remove the Tomatoes from the boiling water and peel the skin away.

3. Seal all of the ingredients by vacuum sealer or the water displacement method.

Cooking you Tomato Confit

1. Pre-heat the Sous Vide to 140°F.

2. Cook the Tomatoes for 40 minutes.

Serving

Serve with Crusty bread and a drizzle of Olive Oil.

Sous Vide Broccoli

Ingredients

- 2 Cups of Broccoli Florets

- 1 Clove of Garlic finely chopped

- 2 Teaspoons of Butter

- Salt and Ground Pepper to taste

Method

1. Seal the Broccoli, Garlic, Butter, Salt and Ground Pepper to taste by vacuum sealer or the water displacement method.

Cooking your Sous Vide Broccoli

1. Pre-heat the Sous Vide to 185°F.

2. Cook the Broccoli for 40 minutes.

Serving

Serve hot with Salmon or steak.

Sweet and Crunchy Onions

Ingredients

- 2 Medium Red Onions cut Julienne
- 1 ½ Tablespoons of Demerara Sugar
- ½ Teaspoon Cumin
- 2 Tablespoons of Olive Oil
- 1 Tablespoon of Balsamic Vinegar
- Salt and Ground Black Pepper to taste

Method

1. Mix the Demerara Sugar, Cumin, Olive Oil, Balsamic Vinegar, Salt, Ground Black Pepper and Onions.
2. Seal the Onion mix by vacuum sealer or water displacement method.

Cooking your Sweet and Crunchy Onions

1. Pre-heat the Sous Vide to 190°F.
2. Cook the Onions for 120 minutes.
3. Remove the Onions and place in an open jar and allow to cool.

OR

For extra crispiness place the Onions in the oven on the middle shelf and cook at 300°F for 15-20 minutes.

Serving

Serve with Salad, Burgers or Hotdogs.

Sweet Potato and Carrot Soup

Ingredients

- 2 Large Sweet Potatoes, peeled and chopped

- 2 Large Carrots, peeled and chopped

- 1 Large Onion, chopped

- 3 Sticks of Celery

- 2 Cloves of Garlic finely chopped

- 1 Teaspoon of Dried Cumin

- 1 Teaspoon of Dried Coriander

- ½ Teaspoon medium heat Chili Powder

- Salt and Ground Black Pepper to taste

- 800ml Chicken Stock

Method

1. Seal the Sweet Potatoes, Carrots, Onion, Celery, Garlic, Cumin, Coriander, Chili Powder and a little Salt and Ground Black Pepper to taste.

Cooking your Sweet Potato and Carrot soup

1. Pre-heat the Sous Vide to 190°F.

2. Cook the Sweet Potato and Carrot mix for 60 minutes.

3. Remove the Sweet Potato and Carrots from the Sous Vide and pour along with the Chicken Stock into a food processor and blend until smooth.

Serving

Serve hot with Crusty Bread.

Spicy carrot and Tomato Soup

Ingredients

- 2 Large Tomatoes, chopped

- 1 Packet of Sun-Dried Tomatoes, chopped

- 2 Large Carrots peeled and chopped

- 1 Red Chili Pepper, chopped

- 1 Large Onion, chopped

- 3 Sticks of Celery

- 2 Cloves of Garlic finely chopped

- 1 Teaspoon of Dried Cumin

- 1 Tablespoon of Tomato Puree

- 1 Teaspoon medium heat Chili Powder

- ½ Teaspoon Paprika

- Salt and Ground Black Pepper to taste

- 800ml Chicken Stock

Method

1. Seal the Tomatoes, Carrots, Onion, Chili Pepper, Celery, Garlic, Cumin, Tomato puree, Chili Powder, Paprika and a little Salt and Ground Black Pepper to taste.

Cooking you Spicy Carrot and Tomato Soup

1. Pre-heat the Sous Vide to 190°F.

2. Cook the Carrot and Tomato for 60 minutes.

3. Remove the Spice Carrot and Tomatoes from the Sous Vide and pour along with the Chicken Stock into a food processor and blend until smooth.

Serving

Serve hot with Crusty Bread.

Lentil Soup

Ingredients

- 2 Cups of Lentils

- 800ml Chicken Stock

- 2 cloves of Garlic finely chopped

- 3 Carrots, peeled and chopped

- 1 Cup of chopped Celery

- 1 White Onion finely chopped

- 1 Tablespoon or Lemon Juice

- ½ Teaspoon of Paprika

- ½ Teaspoon of Cumin

- 1 Teaspoon of Ground Black Pepper

- ¼ Teaspoon of Salt

Method

1. Warm some Olive Oil in a Saucepan and throw in the Garlic, Carrots, Onion, Celery, Salt and Pepper.

2. Cook on a medium heat for 5 minutes.

3. Pour the Chicken Stock, Lentils, Lemon Juice, Paprika, Cumin and the Vegetable mix into a Sous Vide bag and seal by the water displacement method.

Cooking your Lentil Soup

1. Pre-heat the Sous Vide to 180°F.

2. Cook your Lentil and Vegetable mix for 2 hours.

3. Remove from the Sous Vide and pour the Lentil Soup to a large bowl.

Serving

Serve hot with Crusty Bread.

Tomato Soup

Ingredients

- 3 Large Tomatoes, chopped

- 1 Packet of Sun-Dried Tomatoes, chopped

- 1 Cup of Cherry Tomatoes, chopped

- 1 Large Carrot peeled and chopped

- 1 Large Maris Piper or Russets Potato, peeled and chopped

- 1 Red Chili Pepper, chopped

- 2 Cloves of Garlic chopped

- 1 Teaspoon of Dried Cumin

- 2 Tablespoon of Tomato Puree

- 2 Tablespoon Worcestershire Sauce

- Salt and Ground Black Pepper to taste

- 800ml Chicken Stock

Method

1. Seal the Tomatoes, Carrot, Potato, Chili Pepper, Garlic, Cumin, Tomato Puree, Chili Powder and a little Salt and Ground Black Pepper to taste.

Cooking you Tomato Soup

1. Pre-heat the Sous Vide to 190°F.

2. Cook the Tomato for 90 minutes.

3. Remove the Tomato Soup from the Sous Vide and pour along with the Chicken Stock into a food processor and blend until smooth.

Serving

Serve hot with Crusty Bread.

Sous Vide Garlic Roasted Sprouts

Ingredients

- 400g Brussel Sprouts sliced into halves
- 3 Cloves of Garlic finely chopped
- 1 Teaspoon of Mixed Herbs
- 1 Tablespoon of Olive Oil
- Salt and Ground Black Pepper to taste

Method

1. Mix the Garlic, Mixed Herbs, Olive Oil, Salt and Ground Black Pepper in a bowl.
2. Add the Sprout halves and mix well ensuring they are evenly covered.
3. Seal the Sprouts by vacuum sealer or the water displacement method.

Cooking your Sous Vide Garlic Roasted Sprouts

1. Pre-heat your Sous Vide to 180°F.
2. Cook for 30 minutes.
3. Pre-heat the Oven to 300°F.
4. Remove the Sprouts from the Sous Vide and drain the liquid.
5. Put the Sprouts in the Oven and cook for 20 minutes.

Serving

Serve hot with Beef, Pork or Lamb dishes.

Fried Okra

Ingredients

- 400g Okra, sliced into strips

- ½ Cup of Flour

- 1 Teaspoon Paprika

- 1 Teaspoon Cayenne Pepper

- 2 Cloves of Garlic finely chopped

- Salt and Ground Black Pepper

- 1 Cup of Olive Oil

Method

1. Seal the Okra by vacuum sealer or the water displacement method.

2. Mix the Flour, Paprika, Garlic, Cayenne and a little Salt and Ground Black Pepper in a bowl and set the Seasoned Flour Mix to one side.

Cooking your Fried Okra

1. Pre-heat your Sous Vide to 178°F.

2. Cook the Okra for 20 minutes.

3. Pour the Olive Oil into a Saucepan and warm over a medium-high heat.

4. Remove the Okra from the Sous Vide, drain any liquid and pat dry with kitchen towel.

5. Coat the Okra slices in the Seasoned Flour Mix ensure they are all fully and evenly covered.

6. Fry the Okra for 4 minutes or they appear to darken and crisp.

Serving

Serve immediately with Sour Cream Dip.

Maple Parsnips

Ingredients

- 2 Large Parsnips, peeled and sliced into strips

- 1 Tablespoon of Maple Syrup

- 1 Teaspoon of Butter

- Salt and Ground Black Pepper to taste

- Olive Oil

Method

1. Melt the Butter and mix into the Maple Syrup and Salt and Ground Black Pepper to taste.

2. Add the Parsnip strips, ensuring they are fully covered.

3. Seal the Parsnips and any remaining Marinade by vacuum sealer or the water displacement method.

Cooking your Maple Parsnips

1. Pre-heat the Sous Vide to 180°F.

2. Cook the Maple Parsnips for 45 minutes.

Serving

Serve hot with Beef, Fish or Pork dishes.

Fries

Ingredients

- 500g Russet or Maris Piper Potatoes peeled and sliced into Fries
- Salt and Ground Black Pepper
- ½ Cup of Olive Oil

Method

1. Soak the Fries in Water for 10 minutes to remove any excess starch then dry with kitchen towel.

2. Season the Fries with Salt and Ground Black Pepper to taste.

3. Seal the Fries by vacuum sealer or the water displacement method.

Cooking your Fries

1. Pre-heat the sous Vide to 160°F.

2. Cook the Fries for 40-50 minutes.

3. Warm the ½ cup of Olive Oil in a Pan on a medium-high heat.

4. Remove the Fries from the Sous Vide and pat dry with kitchen towel.

5. Carefully place the Fries in the Olive Oil and cook for 8-10 minutes or until golden.

Serving

Serve hot with a sprinkling of Salt.

Sweet Potato Fries

Ingredients

- 500g Sweet Potatoes peeled and sliced into Fries
- Salt and Ground Black Pepper
- 1 ½ Teaspoons of Cumin
- ½ Cup of Olive Oil

Method

1. Soak the Sweet Potato Fries in Water for 10 minutes to remove any excess starch then dry with kitchen towel.
2. Season the Sweet Potato Fries with a sprinkle of Cumin, Salt and Ground Black Pepper to taste.
3. Seal the Sweet Potato Fries by vacuum sealer or the water displacement method.

Cooking your Sweet Potato Fries

1. Pre-heat the Sous Vide to 160°F.
2. Cook the Fries for 40-50 minutes.
3. Warm the ½ cup of Olive Oil in a Pan on a medium-high heat.
4. Remove the Fries from the Sous Vide and pat dry with kitchen towel.
5. Carefully place the Fries in the Olive Oil and cook for 8-10 minutes or until golden.

Serving

Serve hot with a sprinkling of Salt.

Cauliflower Cheese

Ingredients

- 3 Cups of Cauliflower

- 400ml Milk

- 1 ½ Cups of grated Cheddar Cheese

- 1 Tablespoon of Butter

- 1 Tablespoon of Flour

- Salt and Ground black Pepper

Method

1. Season the Cauliflower with some Salt and Ground Black Pepper to taste.

2. Seal the Cauliflower by vacuum sealer or the water displacement method.

Cooking your Cauliflower Cheese

1. Pre-heat the Sous Vide to 185°F.

2. Cook the Cauliflower for 40-50 minutes.

3. 5 Minutes before the Cauliflower is ready melt the butter in a Saucepan over a medium heat.

4. Add the Milk to the butter and stir until the Milk begins to simmer.

5. Lower the heat and begin to add and stir in the grated cheddar a little at a time until melted.

6. If the Cheese Sauce still seems a little watery, add the Flour and stir until the Sauce begins to thicken, add Salt and Ground Black Pepper to taste.

7. Remove the Cauliflower from the Sous Vide, pat dry using kitchen towel and serve.

Serving

Serve hot with a generous pouring of the Cheese Sauce.

DESERTS AND DRINKS

Mulled Wine

Ingredients

- ½ Bottle of Red Wine of choice

- 2 Oranges Peeled + the Peel of 1 Orange

- ¼ Teaspoon of Cinnamon

- 55g Sugar

- 1 Star Anise

- 1 Vanilla Pod sliced in half lengthways

- 1 Clove

- 2 Bay Leaves

Method

1. Pre-heat the Sous Vide to 140°F.

2. Mix all of the ingredients in a large bowl and separate into 2 bags and seal by water displacement method.

3. Place into the Sous Vide and cook for 60 minutes.

4. Remove from the Sous Vide and place the Mulled Wine bags into an ice bath to cool.

5. Strain before serving.

Serving

Allow the Mulled Wine to cool, serve warm.

Spiced Rum

Ingredients

- ½ /bottle of Dark Rum of choice

- 2 Cloves

- 1 Vanilla Pod sliced in half lengthways

- Zest of 1 Orange

- 1 Tablespoon Brown Sugar

- 1 Star Anise

Method

1. Pre-heat the Sous Vide to 140°F.

2. Mix all of the ingredients in a large bowl and separate into 2 bags and seal by water displacement method.

3. Place into the Sous Vide and cook for 90 minutes.

4. Remove from the Sous Vide and place the Spiced Rum bags into an ice bath to cool.

5. Strain before serving.

Serving

Serve with a splash of Water or over Ice.

Deep Burn Chili Vodka

Ingredients

- ½ Bottle of Vodka

- 3 Red Chilies sliced in half

Method

1. Pre-heat the Sous Vide to 140°F.

2. Mix the Chilies and Vodka in a large bowl and separate into 2 bags and seal by water displacement method.

3. Place into the Sous Vide and cook for 90 minutes.

4. Remove from the Sous Vide and place the Deep Burn Chili Vodka bags into an ice bath to cool.

5. Strain before serving.

Serving

Serve when cool over Ice with a slice of Lemon.

Raspberry Vodka

Ingredients

- 300g Raspberries

- 1½ Cup of Sugar

- 2 Tablespoons of Lemon Juice

- 70cl Bottle of Vodka

Method

1. Pre-heat the Sous Vide to 140°F.

2. Mix the Raspberries, Lemon Juice, and Sugar in a bowl, crush the Raspberries with the back of a wooden spoon. When the Raspberries have been mashed ad the Vodka, stir and separate into 2 bags and seal by water displacement method.

3. Place into the Sous Vide and cook for 90 minutes.

4. Remove from the Sous Vide and place the Raspberry Vodka bags into an ice bath to cool.

5. Strain before serving.

Serving

Serve cool with Ice.

Spiced Apple Cider

Ingredients

- 1 Litre of Cider

- 1 Tablespoon of Honey

- 1 Vanilla Pod slice in half lengthways

- 1 Cinnamon Stick

- ½ Teaspoon of Pepper Corns

- 2 Teaspoons of Orange Juice

- 2 Tablespoons of Lemon Juice

Method

1. Pre-heat the Sous Vide to 140°F.

2. Mix the Cider, Honey, Cinnamon, Pepper Corns and Lemon juice in a large bowl and separate into 2 bags and seal by water displacement method.

3. Place into the Sous Vide and cook for 60 minutes.

4. Remove from the Sous Vide and place the Spiced Apple Cider bags into an ice bath to cool.

5. Strain before serving.

Serving

Allow to cool, serve warm.

Orange Liquor

Ingredients

- 2 Large cups of Brandy of Choice

- Zest of 6 large Oranges

- 4 Tablespoons of Orange Juice

- 1 Tablespoon of Honey

Method

1. Pre-heat the Sous Vide to 180°F.

2. Mix all of the ingredients in a large mixing bowl, then separate into 2 Sous Vide Bags and seal by the water displacement method.

3. Cook the Orange Liquor for 90 minutes.

4. Cool by placing the Orange Liquor bags into an Ice bath.

5. Strain before serving.

Serving

Serve cool over Ice.

Elderberry Cordial Syrup

Ingredients

- 250g Dried Elderberries

- 15ml Grape Concentrate

- 2 Cups of Water

- 1 Cup of Sugar

- 2 Tablespoons of Lemon Juice

Method

1. Pre-heat the Sous Vide to 135°F.

2. Mix all of the ingredients in a bowl and then separate into 2 Sous Vide bags and seal by the water displacement method.

3. Cook for 90 minutes.

4. Remove from the Sous Vide and strain the Elderberry cordial into a Saucepan on a medium heat and stir the Elderberry Cordial until it reduces by 50%.

Serving

When cool serve with Water and Ice, 1 part Elderberry Cordial Syrup to 5 parts Water.

Home Made Yoghurt

Ingredients

- 1 Litre of Cows Milk

- 3 Tablespoons of full fat Yoghurt with Live Active Cultures

Method

1. Pre-heat the Sous Vide to 115°F.

2. Pour the Milk into jars (leaving room to add Yoghurt) and place into the Sous Vide and increase the heat of the Sous Vide to 180°F.

3. Cook for 30 minutes.

4. After 30 minutes, lower the Sous Vide temperature to 112°F.

5. Add the Yoghurt to the milk jars in the Sous Vide and cook of 12 hours.

6. Lower the Sous Vide temperature to room temperature and leave for 60 minutes.

7. Remove the jars of Yoghurt from the Sous Vide and place in the fridge for at least 3 hours.

Serving

Serve with Honey.

Sous Vide Strawberry Compote

Ingredients

- 200g Strawberries, sliced

- 4 Tablespoon of Sugar

- 2 Tablespoons of Lemon Juice

- 2 Tablespoons of Balsamic Vinegar

Method

1. Pre-heat the Sous Vide to 184°F.

2. Mix the Sugar, Lemon, Balsamic Vinegar and Strawberries in a bowl, ensure the mix is fully combined and that the Strawberries are fully coated.

3. Seal the Strawberries by vacuum sealer or the water displacement method.

4. Cook the Strawberries for 18 minutes.

Serving

Serve, warm as a topping for Ice Cream or Yoghurt.

Sous Vide Raspberry Compote

Ingredients

- 200g Raspberries

- 4 Tablespoons of Sugar

- 2 Tablespoons of Lemon Juice

- 2 Tablespoons of Balsamic Vinegar

Method

1. Pre-heat the Sous Vide to 184°F.

2. Mix the Sugar, Lemon, Balsamic Vinegar and Raspberries in a bowl, ensure the mix is fully combined and that the Strawberries are fully coated.

3. Seal the Raspberries by vacuum sealer or the water displacement method.

4. Cook the Raspberries for 18 minutes.

Serving

Serve, warm as a topping for Ice Cream or Yoghurt.

Brandy Pears

Ingredients

- 4 Pears, peeled and halved

- 1 Cup of Brandy of choice

- 1 Cinnamon Stick

Method

1. Seal the Pears, Brandy and Cinnamon Stick by the water displacement method.

Cooking your Brandy Pears

1. Pre-heat the Sous Vide to 90°F.

2. Cook the Pears for 30 minutes.

Serving

Serve hot with Ice Cream, Home Made Yoghurt, Honey and a splash of the Brandy.

Vanilla Cinnamon Pears

Ingredients

- 4 Asian Pears halved and cored.

- 4 Tablespoons of Honey

- ¼ Cup White Wine

- 2 Tablespoons of Butter

- 2 Vanilla Pods sliced lengthways

- 1 Teaspoon of Cinnamon

Method

1. Mix all of the ingredients in a bowl, separate into 2 Sous Vide bags and seal using the water displacement method.

Cooking your Vanilla Cinnamon Pears

2. Pre-heat the Sous Vide to 180°F.

3. Cook the Pears for 90 minutes.

4. Remove the Pears from the Sous Vide and put to one side.

5. Pour the liquid into a Saucepan on a medium heat and stir until the liquid has reduced by half.

Serving

Serve hot with Ice Cream and a drizzle of the cooking sauce.

Strawberry Mousse

Ingredients

- 500g Strawberries

- ¼ Cup of Brown Sugar

- ½ Teaspoon Salt

- ¼ Teaspoon of Cinnamon

- 1 Cup of Full Cream

- 1 Cup of Crème Fraiche

- 2 Tablespoons of Lemon Juice

- 1 Tablespoon of Lime Juice

- ½ Teaspoon of Vanilla Essence

Method

1. Pre-heat the Sous Vide to 182°F.

2. Seal the Strawberries, Sugar, Salt and cinnamon by vacuum sealer or the water displacement method.

3. Cook the Strawberries for 45 minutes.

4. Remove the Strawberries from the Sous Vide and blend until smooth using either a Blender or a Food Processor and allow to cool.

5. In a large mixing bowl whisk the Full Cream and Vanilla essence until it forms stiff peaks.

6. Evenly fold the Strawberries and Crème Fraiche into the whipped cream.

7. Refrigerate for at least 30 minutes before serving.

Serving

Serve in a chilled bowl.

Raspberry Mousse

Ingredients

- 500g Raspberries

- ¼ Cup of Brown Sugar

- ½ Teaspoon Salt

- ¼ Teaspoon of Cinnamon

- 1 Cup of Full Cream

- 1 Cup of Crème Fraiche

- 2 Tablespoons of Lemon Juice

- 1 Tablespoon of Lime Juice

- 2 Vanilla Pods cut in half lengthways

Method

1. Pre-heat the Sous Vide to 182°F.

2. Seal the Raspberries, Sugar, Salt and cinnamon by vacuum sealer or the water displacement method.

3. Cook the Raspberries for 45 minutes.

4. Remove the Raspberries from the Sous Vide and blend until smooth using either a Blender or a Food Processor and allow to cool.

5. In a large mixing bowl whisk the Full Cream and Vanilla essence until it forms stiff peaks.

6. Evenly fold the Raspberries and Crème Fraiche into the whipped cream.

7. Refrigerate for at least 30 minutes before serving.

Serving

Serve in a chilled bowl.

Strawberry Jam

Ingredients

- 2 Cups of Strawberries

- 1 Large cup of Sugar

- 2 Tablespoon of Lemon Juice

- 2 Tablespoon of powdered Pectin

Method

1. Pre-heat the Sous Vide to 180°F.

2. Seal all of the ingredients by vacuum sealer or the water displacement method.

3. Cook the Strawberries for 90 minutes.

4. Remove the Raspberries and Apples from the Sous Vide and when cool transfer to an airtight container.

Serving

Delicious on Toast or as Yoghurt topping.

Raspberry and Apple Jam

Ingredients

- 1 ½ Cups of Raspberries

- ½ Cup of chopped Apple

- 1 Large cup of Sugar

- 2 Tablespoon of Lemon Juice

- 2 Tablespoon of powdered Pectin

Method

1. Pre-heat the Sous Vide to 180°F.

2. Seal all of the ingredients by vacuum sealer or the water displacement method.

3. Cook the Raspberries and Apples for 90 minutes.

4. Remove the Raspberries and Apples from the Sous Vide and when cool transfer to an airtight container.

Serving

Delicious on Toast or as Yoghurt topping.

Sous Vide Bloody Mary

Ingredients

- 3 Cups of Vodka

- 2 Large Tomatoes, diced

- 1 Packet of Sun-Dried Tomatoes

- 1 Red Pepper, chopped

- 1 Teaspoon of Peppercorns

- 2 Chili Peppers, chopped

- 2 Clovers if Garlic, halved

- Zest of 1 Lemon

- Zest of 1 Lime

Method

1. Pre-heat the Sous Vide to 145°F.

2. Mix all of the ingredients in a large bowl and separate into 2 Sous Vide bags and seal by the water displacement method.

3. Cook the Bloody Marys for 2 hours and 45 minutes.

4. Cool the Bloody Marys by placing the Sous Vide bags into an Ice Bath.

5. Strain before serving.

Serving

Serve chilled over Ice.

Tomato Shrub

Ingredients

- 1 Cup of Tomatoes, diced

- 1 Pack Sun-Dried Tomatoes, diced

- 2 Cups of Sugar

- 2 Cups of Red Wine Vinegar

- 2 Tablespoons of Lemon Juice

- 1 Cup of Water

Method

1. Pre-heat the Sous Vide to 178°F.

2. Mix all of the ingredients in a large bowl and separate into 2 Sous Vide bags and seal by the water displacement method.

3. Cook the Tomato Shrub for 90 minutes.

4. Cool the Tomato Shrub by placing the Sous Vide bags into an Ice Bath.

5. Strain before serving.

Serving

1. Serve cold with Ice.

2. Serve cold with a shot of Rum or Brandy.

Bacon Infused Bourbon Liquor

Ingredients

- 3 Cups of Bourbon

- 2 Whole Cloves

- 1 Pack of Smoked Bacon

- 3 Tablespoon of Brown Sugar

Method

1. Fry the Bacon until crisp.

2. Pre-heat the Sous Vide to 150°F.

3. Seal all of the ingredients including the Bacon and 3 Tablespoon of the Bacon Fat saved cooking by vacuum sealer or the water displacement method.

4. Cook the Bourbon and Bacon for 60 minutes.

5. Remove the Bacon Infused Bourbon Liquor from the Sous Vide and strain into a bowl, allow to cool.

6. Once the Bacon Infused Bourbon Liquor has cooled to room temperature place it in the refrigerator for 2 hours or until any Bacon Fat has solidified on the surface.

7. Remove any solidified Fat and strain the Bacon Infused Bourbon Liquor through a Cheesecloth and Sieve.

Serving

Serve chilled over Ice.

Sous Vide Apple Sauce

Ingredients

- 2 Large Cooking Apples peeled and sliced

- ½ Cup of Sugar

- 1 Tablespoon of Lemon Juice

Method

1. Seal the Apples, sugar and Lemon Juice by vacuum sealer or the water displacement method.

Cooking your Sous Vide Apple Sauce

1. Pre-heat the Sous Vide to 180°F.

2. Cook the Sous Vide Apple Sauce for 40 minutes.

3. Remove the Apple Sauce from the Sous Vide, pour into a serving bowl and lightly mash.

Serving

Serve with Pork dishes.

Poached Apples

Ingredients

- 4-6 Golden Delicious or Granny Smith Apples, cored and peeled

- 1 Tablespoon on Lemon Juice

- 1 Shot of Rum

- 2 Tablespoons of Brown Sugar

- ¼ Teaspoon Cinnamon

- ¼ Teaspoon Cardamom

- 1 Whole Clove cut in half

Method

1. Mix the Lemon Juice, Rum, Brown Sugar Cinnamon, Cardamom and Clove in a bowl.

2. Seal the Apple and mix by vacuum sealer or the water displacement method.

Cooking your Poached Apples

1. Pre-heat the Sous Vide to 170°F.

2. Cook the Apples for 40-50 minutes.

Serving

Serve hot with your favourite Ice Cream and a drizzle of the cooking liquid.